2 Book Bundle – This Book Includes:

Essential Beginner's Guide to Seeing, Feeling, and Knowing

Tips and Tricks to Reading People and Energy Fields

By Valerie W. Holt

Contents

Auras

Essential Beginner's Guide to Seeing, Feeling, and Knowing

By Valerie W. Holt

Introduction

The following chapters will discuss the basics of what an aura is and how anyone, including you, can learn to see, feel, and know auras. It might seem overwhelming at first, but this book will show you how to develop your natural gifts so you too can read auras.

There are plenty of books on this subject on the market, thanks again for choosing this one! Every effort was made to ensure it is full of as much useful information as possible; please enjoy!

Chapter 1

What are Auras

Most of us have been in a situation in which auras have been casually brought up in the conversation. Many people are left wondering what an aura is and what they mean. This confusion generally stems from a lack of understanding, and with so many different ideas about what an aura is, this is understandable. However, like most anything else, all it takes is a little education to make things much clearer. If you know about auras, the next time it is brought up in conversation you will have some correct information to share. You might also find that a lot of people will be very curious to hear what you have to say. There are many people interested in auras and aura reading than what you may think. There are still skeptics out there who make some people hesitant to ask questions or seek out information on their own.

On a fundamental level, it is the magnetic field surrounding every living thing that makes up an aura. A person's aura is unique and reflects their own particular energy; it is this energy that impacts their capacity to connect and interact with others. Most people's auras extend about three feet around them, but those who have suffered a tragedy or a trauma usually have a larger aura. Much of what we do in our lives leave some mark on our aura, that is why experienced readers can tell so much about a person during a reading. Our aura is so intimately connected to both our minds and our bodies, that it is difficult to keep secrets from experienced readers. This is why it is good to choose a reader than you think you can trust and that you feel comfortable with.

The study of chakras is an ancient tradition and was often treated more like a visit to a doctor. It was known that the chakras held information about both our mental and physical health, so it would make sense to see someone about chakra alignment if there was an issue. Our auras originate from these chakras and therefore, can also reveal what ails us. Many people believe that getting regular aura readings keeps them healthy because the aura can reflect some diseases or illnesses before more classic symptoms arise, increasing the likelihood of a speedy and full recovery.

Experienced aura readers do not even need to meet their subject in person to give a proper reading; they can just do it from a normal photograph. That is how deeply connected we are to our auras, they show up in regular photographs, meaning they must be pretty powerful for that to happen. Auras can always change, because they reflect our thoughts and emotions, so while some of the basic traits, both and good and bad remain the same, other aspects of our aura shift along with our moods and circumstances.

An aura is not one single unit. Instead, it is made up of many different layers. The aura's layers interconnect and mingle that form the cohesive body that is known as the aura. Each layer of the aura holds different types of information, these are known as the subtle bodies. The energy created by the chakras are what create the auras. The size of a person's aura depends on their spiritual, emotional, and physical health; these auric layers will contract or increase depending on these facets.

The 7 Layers That Make Up an Aura:

The first layer also called the etheric layer remains close to the body, generally only extending an inch or two from the body. The etheric field reflects your physical health and is usually different shades blue. This layer will change shade and radius along with your physical health. This layer originates from the root chakra, and it is what makes up the link between your physical and higher bodies.

The second layer that is influenced by emotions generally extends only about one to three inches from the body. This layer holds your emotions and feelings, which we all know change on a regular basis depending on your particular circumstances. Usually, this layer is bright and combines many different colors, but negative feelings and emotions can act as a block which can dull or darken the color. The sacral chakra is associated with this layer, which is fitting because it is the heart's location, the figurative source of emotion.

The third layer of the aura is the mental field, and it can spread out from the body anywhere from three to eight inches. The mental layer is generally a shade of yellow, varying from bright to dull. For those suffering from depression or anxiety, this layer is greatly affected. This layer also relates to the solar plexus chakra.

The fourth layer is the astral layer, which acts a bridge to the spiritual realm and is connected to the astral plane. This layer extends about a foot from the body and contains all the colors of the rainbow, with the brightness correlating with a person's spiritual health. The astral plane is one part of the multi-dimensional planes that surrounds us. This plane vibrates at a higher frequency than the physical plane that we live in. The fourth layer is connected with the heart or fourth chakra and is often referred to as the 'layer of love' for this reason. It also joins the higher three and lower three auric layers.

The fifth layer is called the etheric template; it protrudes around two feet from the body. This layer contains a guideline of the entities in the physical world, and because of this it is not usually associated with a specific color. This layer can also create negative space because it does deal with the physical world, but this is not negative; it just means that many different colors can be associated with it. The throat or fifth chakra is related to this layer and represents your personality and identity.

The sixth layer is also known as the celestial aura and can protrude up to two and a half feet from the body. This layer is also linked to the spiritual realm and any communication with that realm is reflected in this layer. The celestial aura also mirrors feelings of ecstasy and unconditional love. The colors in this layer appear shimmery and are usually pearly pastels. This layer originates from the third eye or sixth chakra, intuition and perception are the focus here.

The final layer can extend up to three feet from the body and is known as the ketheric layer. This field contains all the other layers and basically, acts as a barrier to hold them together. The ketheric layer vibrates at the highest frequencies and contains bright gold threads that weave throughout it. This layer reflects the trials and experiences that have made an impact on the soul. The ketheric layer acts as your own personal connection to the Divine and aids in your journey of being personally connected to the universe. The crown chakra is related to this layer, and it represents our connection with all that exists.

Even though these layers all make up the aura, the first layer itself is not actually the aura; it is the energy that leads to the creation of the aura. This is also known as the energosma, and the aura really starts where the energosma ends, which is why auras can vary in size from person to person and from day to day. As our emotions and thoughts change, so do our auras. They are a manifestation of our overall health.

One person's aura can also be affected by another person's, this is known as an auric connection and can make communication easier. This happens because the energies from the two people become stronger and take on a greater role in the communication, usually without the people knowing it is even happening. This helps to explain those inexplicable connections we have with some people as if we have known them for years.

When it comes to reading auras, there is no one right way. They all deal with psychic abilities and some people will be more naturally inclined to one or more and may choose only to pursue that which comes easier to them. The ways to read auras include seeing, feeling, and knowing them, they are all similar and even connected in some ways, but all are equally effective. So when you decide which path to pursue, you might decide to choose feeling because you are someone who already depends on your sense of intuition. Opting to develop further what is already a natural psychic gift will make the process easier since it is already something you have used and at least somewhat developed even if you are not consciously aware of doing so.

Just like the human body, auras are complex. They are direct reflections of how we feel at any given time. Even if we are not aware of it, our auras can show those capable of reading them how we are feeling about our lives and how our past experiences have impacted us. As we grow and evolve, so will our aura, since it is basically a mirror of what we are feeling on the inside. This means that if you want a brighter aura, there are things you can do to make that happen.

Chapter 2

How to See Auras

The aura is usually seen in the shape of an oval around a person; it can range from seeming brighter, glossier, or more polished in that area. Some people describe texture or vibration changes within the aura area as well, but this is not always the case. Some people may see only bright white, while others can see specific colors of a person's aura, others might not even see colors at all. When you are first learning to see auras, it will probably tend to be relatively motionless as well.

Everyone has the potential to be able to see auras, just like any other muscle in the body, it needs to be worked and nurtured to be strengthened. In reference to auras, the sense you will be focusing on is your natural clairvoyant abilities, because this is what will give you the ability to see auras.

Clairvoyance is known as a psychic ability, but not in the most traditional sense, in terms of auras, it just means that you are learning to perceive something beyond the traditional physical senses. To see auras, you will depend on your ability to see the astral body, which as you know operates on a higher frequency than the physical world, hence the connection to clairvoyant abilities.

Tapping into this new sense requires patience, even though we all have the innate ability to see auras, our brains have been conditioned to repress this ability since it is not often used or accepted. That means the people who can read and see auras are not that different than the rest of us, they have just learned not to repress their natural psychic abilities and have embraced and practiced them instead. However, seeing auras and colors is not the only method, it is just one of the most common.

The first step in being able to see auras is to understand where clairvoyant abilities come from. They can be triggered by times of extreme stress and trauma, but this is generally short-lived and is not controlled. The best and most reliable psychic abilities come from a place of calm and alignment, which can often be achieved through regular meditation and awareness. So before you attempt to see auras, find a place of calm mental clarity because it will help to increase your chances of success.

Seeing Auras:

Small Start - As mentioned in the first chapter, all living things have an aura, so when you first start, it is better to choose something more simple, such as a plant. Plants are perfect for improving the reading of auras, especially for beginners. So, choose a plant, make sure to choose one that will not move in the wind and find a comfortable and quiet place to sit.

Vision – Once you have found your quiet location and chosen a stationary plant, go through your relaxation techniques to find you inner calm. When you feel confident and comfortable, focus on the top of the plant. Gently relax your eyes and allow them to go slightly out of focus. Some might find this difficult, so if you find you are having problems with this technique, imagine an invisible leaf and focus on that specific leaf instead.

Perception – Learning to extend your visual perception is the most difficult part, it takes patience and practice, so if you don't get it the first time, don't get discouraged. A plant's aura will not be colorful because thoughts and emotions create the colors of an aura, so look for the glossier, or brightness surrounding it. To do this successfully, keep your focus on the top of the plant, but allow your visual perception, with your eyes slightly out of focus, to take in the plant and its surrounding area. Eventually, you will be able to see its aura as well, once your natural clairvoyant ability kicks in, after all, it has been lying dormant for so long, it will take some time for it to make itself known and even more time for you to learn to control it.

Mirror – When you feel confident that you have seen the plant's aura, it is time to move to something a bit more challenging. You will be using the same technique that you used with the plant but on your own aura. So find a nice quiet area, a large mirror that allows you to see your top half, place a light source on each side of the mirror, and sit in a comfortable position. Make sure the light sources do not cause a reflection in the mirror, as this can distort the aura making it more difficult for you to give a proper reading. Adjust your eyes and allow them to go slightly out of focus while looking at your own reflection in the mirror, focus on a spot above one of your shoulders. After some time, you will begin to see a slight glow around your head or even the rest of your body. What you are seeing is your energosoma, or your energetic body.

Practice – In the last step, you were able to see the first layer of your aura, which is the easiest part of the aura to see. Practice seeing this field as often as possible; this will increase your clairvoyant ability and give you a greater sense of controlling it. When you can easily see the base layer, gradually shift your focus a little further from the body to see the most subtle parts of the aura itself. Your visual perception will grow the more you practice, meaning you will be able to see more and more of your own aura.

Partner – Once you can comfortably shift your visual perception when it comes to your own aura, it is time to challenge yourself by seeing someone else's aura. When you are beginning it helps to ask someone that you know well and are comfortable with, instead of a casual acquaintance. Again, choose a quiet location with a lightly colored blank wall and ask them to stand about 18 inches in front of it.

Use the same technique you used to see your own aura with the mirror. Do not focus on their eyes, instead, look passed where they are standing and allow your eyes to go slightly out of focus. Just as you did not look directly at yourself in the mirror, ignore their body as well and let your visual perception extend passed them to take in their aura. If you can only see the base layer as a subtle glow, in the beginning, that is okay. It can seem strange or odd trying to see someone else's aura for the first time, so take your time and remain calm. Allow your vision to sweep the area around their body and take note of any subtle color differences, that is why a white wall is ideal since it will allow you to see the subtle color differences. Ask them to slowly sway from side to side and practice keeping your eyes from focusing. With practice, as the person sways you will be able to see the color differences better because as the person's energy moves, so will the colors in their aura.

Once you have finished with this make sure you discuss what you felt and saw with the person. My book, _Auras: Tips and Tricks for Reading People and Energy Fields_ will go in depth about colors and their corresponding meanings, but you should still talk about what you saw with them. Tips:

- Letting your eyes go slightly out of focus will come naturally to some, but for others, it will require practice. The best way to describe the proper way to do this is to use something many of us remember using as children. Many of us were fascinated by 3-D stereogram pictures, also known as Magic Eyes, where an image is hidden in the 'noise' of the initial picture. At first glance, the picture might just look like identical and repetitive pineapples or kites, but when you relaxed your eyes, a 3-D shark or butterfly was revealed. The way your eyes would relax to see the image is what you want to do when seeing auras. Even if it doesn't come easily, with practice, you will learn to control it.

- When you are learning to see auras, the colors will probably be very faint, and you might be convinced that they are not there at all. There is a trick to help you see even the faintest of colors, though. You will need colored construction paper and white poster board to do this. Cut out circles of the following colors: red, yellow, orange, pink, blue, purple, green, and black. Place one of the circles on the white piece of poster board and stare at it for at least 30 seconds, then quickly remove it and continue to stare at the poster board. You will see the opposite color of the circle you were staring at; this is known as an afterimage. Relax your eyes, and you will discover that your eyes focus deeper than the surface of the poster board, this is the same as seeing auras. Continue to do this will all of the colors, and repeat it often. Doing so will increase your visual perception by allowing you to see more colors within auras.

- Remember that everyone's aura is different, so keep an open mind. Not everyone will have the same glow around them, but that does not mean you have suddenly lost your ability, it just means that they have a different energy which produces a different color. When this happens, it is usually connected to a person's base personality.

- Remember to be patient. This cannot be stressed enough. It takes a while to master a skill, and this is no different. Try not to be too hard on yourself, because that will cause you additional stress. The best and most controlled clairvoyant abilities come from inner calmness and tranquility, being frustrated and stressed is not going to help achieve that. Instead of getting aggravated with a lack of progress, celebrate the small victories and keep practicing.

- It will not do you any good to try to force yourself to do something that doesn't feel natural to you at all. There are many different ways of seeing or sensing an aura; it does not have to involve color at all. So if you find yourself hitting a wall after months of trying with no results, then you might want to try a different technique. You are born with the potential to read auras; you just need to find what works for you.

- Do not compare your journey to others, this is unhealthy and will just hinder your progress. You want to keep a positive and open attitude when entering into the world of aura reading, this will not only make it more fun for you, but it will also make the process more enjoyable overall. That is how it should be; it is something new and fun, do your best to keep it that way.

- Remember to start small and pace yourself. Make sure you are confident and comfortable in your skills before you progress. There is nothing wrong with taking your time and perfecting your skills, after all, you can practice on yourself. There is also the added bonus of getting to yourself better throughout the process.

- There are different exercises that you can do to help you connect with your psychic gifts so don't be afraid to take advantage of them. Two of the most popular exercises are meditation and mindful thinking. Learning to let go of negative thoughts and focus on the here and now helps you to channel the more nontraditional senses. Practicing mindful thinking gives you control of your thoughts, helping you cope with life's stressors more productively and healthily giving your mind more room for positive thinking.

Not everyone is interested in reading auras, and that is okay, just know that if you are, you can be successful. If you practice on a regular basis and believe in what you are doing, then you will begin to see results. Everything in the universe has its own energy and vibration; you are just learning to see certain vibrations for the first time. Think of it regarding this: imagine walking around outside on a bright and sunny day, and then walking into a pitch-black room. To see anything, your eyes will need time to adjust, but even that isn't enough to allow you to see everything through the darkness, for that to happen you will need some form of illumination. Learning to read auras is like looking for the light switch, and then successfully being able to see or sense them is that light turning on. Your world is still the same, it is just brighter, and you have a better grasp of your surroundings.

Learning to see auras might seem daunting, but it can actually be a fun and rewarding journey. You will learn more about yourself and develop a deeper connection to the Divine and the spiritual realm by doing so. Just the act of connecting to your inner clairvoyant abilities will increase your sense of self and your awareness of the world around you.

Chapter 3

How to Feel Auras

It is not necessary to see auras to read them some people are more predisposed to feeling rather than seeing when it comes to natural psychic abilities. Learning to feel auras might be more appropriate for you if you are more sensitive to general feelings of intuition, such as just receiving a negative feeling from walking into a room without being able to pinpoint the reason or being uncomfortable around a person, for no specific reason. Most people call this 'going with their gut,' and believe it or not; it is also a basic psychic ability.

Just as you can train yourself to see auras, you can also learn to feel auras as well. Auras are created by energy and energy can be felt just as it is seen. Each of the layers of an aura is capable of being felt by those who are sensitive to it. At some point, you have probably felt or sensed someone staring at you; this is the same concept. No movement made you feel that way; it was the energy that you felt which alerted you to the feeling. It is the aura that picks up this information, to begin with, so that being said, there is no reason why the aura itself cannot be felt just as much as being seen.

The first step in learning to feel auras is to learn to feel energy fields. Just like learning to see auras, it is best to start small and work your way up gradually. The following is a technique to develop this ability:

1. Find a location where you sit comfortably in front of a blank wall. Dim the lights or use a candle for subtle lighting. Close your eyes and find an inner calm by taking some deep breaths.

2. Sensitize your nerve fibers by rubbing your hands together for at least 30 seconds. You

will feel heat, vibrations, or even tingling right after, this is meant to happen and is all part of the process.

3. Stretch your arms out in front of you with open, but slightly cupped hands, as if you are holding a giant invisible ball, but your arms should be mostly straight.

4. Begin with your hands about three feet apart and slowly bring them together as if you are holding the ball in front of your heart. Slowly move them together and apart. You will need to do this a few times to get the hang of it because it can feel like an awkward movement when you are first starting out.

5. Pay attention to any resistance, friction, or any other sensations you feel when you begin moving your hands. Pay close attention to any differences you feel when they are closer together as opposed to further apart. You

might feel a slight pull when they get closer together and a release when they are further apart. The energy field is what creates the resistance, in this case, it is your heart chakra because your hands are in front of your chest.

6. Visualize your hands coming together to hold the invisible ball and separating. Let your inner visual perception take over; this is known as clairsentience because it is about feeling rather than seeing. You might feel a color or a glow as your hands get closer together near your chest. For some, there is an even an added physicality added to the feeling such as tingling, a slight vibration, or a pulsing; this is your own energy field that you are feeling.

7. Continue to do this daily, but focus on different parts of the body. Allow yourself to feel the rest of your own energy and extend this passed an initial couple of inches from the

body. Allow yourself to gradually feel outward and sense the glow and colors associated with what you sense.

Once you feel comfortable feeling your own energy field and aura, you can easily move on to sensing the auras of other people as well using the same technique. In the traditional sense, the feeling is associated with touch. Feeling auras is not really different, only instead of physically touching, you are using your energy to feel, but the hands are still an important part of this.

Practicing Your Perceptions:

Find someone you know and are comfortable with, because this exercise is going to help you sense someone else's aura. Just as you felt the push and pull between your own hands from your own energy field and aura, you can do the same with someone else's. The reason for choosing someone you are comfortable with is because this is a rather intimate experience since you will probably also feel what they are feeling. For instance, if they are going some issues in their life, you might feel heaviness, sluggishness, or even a prickliness and if you are close to the person, it will be easier to talk about what you felt when you are finished.

Choose an environment similar to the one you practiced in, but have the person sit in a chair with their eyes closed. Stand directly behind them and rub your hands together for at least 30 seconds to open the fibers necessary for the exercise. Keeping your eyes open run your hands close to their body without directly touching them. You want to feel their energy and run your hands through their aura, but not directly touch them. Do not run your hands over their head either, just from the shoulders down.

Move your hands around your body slowly step back and pay close attention to any differences in sensations. Remember how you were holding the invisible ball, imagine doing the same, but with the body of the person sitting in front of you. You want to sense each layer of their aura so step back at least three feet and pay attention to any differences in this area as well. Continue to run your hands around them while continuously moving closer and further away from their body.

Just as you did with yourself, make a note of any sensations you feel. Perhaps, you can sense a glow or a color shift the closer you get to them, or maybe you feel tingles when you get further away. Pay attention to when and where you feel the different sensations and try to separate them into their corresponding layers. For instance, maybe you feel more resistance in about eight inches from the body, meaning the third layer or the mental layer.

Now stand directly behind them and hold your hands above their head, palms facing inwards towards the head. Close your eyes and allow yourself to feel. This spot holds a strong connection to the aura, and you will be able to feel the most from here. Let your inner intuition lead you through feeling their aura. Note all the feelings that you feel through your connected energies. You might even see flashes of images in your mind, make a note of them so they can be discussed later and continue to absorb everything their aura is telling you.

Move your fingers to the top of their head, and focus on any new sensations. This is the crown chakra, and it holds spiritual ideals, and therefore much insight. Take your time doing this and pay special attention to even the smallest sensations. This is about feeling, so try to feel what their aura is reflecting, let your energy pull theirs in to give you the information you seek. Feel for any changes in emotion or even any physical changes as well such as coldness or tingles. Without jumping to conclusions, make a note of any mental impressions you received, for now, you just need to feel them, not interpret what they mean.

Once you feel comfortable ending the session, discuss what you felt with the other person. Start by asking them if they felt anything when you were running your hands through their aura. Some people might not understand what you mean, so be sure to explain that it can be as subtle as a slight tingle or a feeling of resistance. Once you have an understanding of what they felt, you can describe to them what you felt. If you felt any specific emotions such as sluggishness, ask them why they think you might have felt that particular emotion. If you felt something in a specific layer discuss the things that layer corresponds with, a previous example was the mental layer, so if you felt a sensation in that layer ask them about what they have been going through that might have caused a disturbance in that specific field.

Chances are, you probably had flashes of color in your mind's eye during the exercise. Auras deal with colors, and those flashes that you received would match that of someone's reading who could see auras. So even though you do not see the colors with your eyes, you are still sensing them. When you are first learning to sense auras, it is a good idea to keep a journal of the sensations you feel both yours and others. When you learn to interpret what they mean, it will make it easier for you to have a reference point to go back to if you don't remember something. When dealing with psychic abilities, even the smallest things can be important so having a detailed journal helps you keep track of everything.

This might not come easily to you in the beginning, but the more you practice and dedicate time to it, the easier it will become. There are ways to develop this sense throughout your day that does not involve a one-on-one experience. For those who are especially sensitive to feelings, they can have a hard time in large groups because they are overwhelmed with a lot of emotions they are sensing. If you are not one of these people but wish to feel more, the next time you walk into a room pay attention to every small sensation and emotion swirling around you. It is often called a 'vibe' that people pick up on, and believe it or not most just choose to ignore it. However, you have the power to focus on it and let yourself feel everything.

Strengthen this by staying in the moment. Train yourself to stop for a minute and just absorb what you feel around you just as you did with your hands and your own energy. Take the time to feel as much as you can wherever you are. The more you do this, the more you will be able to pick up on, and it will make feeling auras come much easier to you. It is not as difficult as people think it is to develop their psychic abilities. Most people depend on them much more than they realize, so they are already there, you just need to be able to tap into them when you choose to without an outside trigger.

Chapter 4

How to Know Auras

There is a lot to know about auras since they are so complex and unique to the individual. They are as unique as fingerprints and exist whether we know it or not. When dealing with the spiritual realm or the Divine, some people are skeptical and do not believe in such things. Regardless if someone believes in it or not, it is still real. Being educated about auras helps you to identify what they truly mean, that they are more than just a collection of colors. They are created from who we are as individuals, made up of our thoughts, emotions, behaviors, experiences, and ideas.

To know an aura, you must not assume that what you see is everything and that it is permanent. Just as a person's thoughts and emotions change so does their aura. So what is seen one day might not be true the next. Some aura readers never see colors at all but are excellent readers because they use other psychic abilities that allow them to receive the same information. Color is important, but it is not necessary to see colors to be a successful aura reader. The information you seek as a reader is not just shown in colors, our energy and vibration are much more powerful than that, after all, it is magnificent enough to create an aura in the first place. Learning to trust your gifts and strengths will make you more successful than trying to force yourself to do something that doesn't feel natural.

Aura reading is also more than just seeing what is offered to you on the surface. There is more to it than just positive or negative 'vibes.' Think of it in terms of literacy; you need to know how to understand and interpret what is given to you. There is a difference between a vague statement that could be true for nearly anyone and a detailed, knowing reading that is based on depth and detail. The best and most experienced readers know that what they see on the surface is not the whole story. They also know that an aura represents a map of many different things we have done throughout our lives, some of which will leave a permanent mark, while others are fleeting. It is important to differentiate between the two, but both are still important.

Auras are directly related to Chakras which have studied for thousands of years, the word itself is ancient Sanskrit. Each of the chakras contains about 50 different types of stored information. That is a lot of information about the human body including emotions, physical health, character traits, even consumer concerns. This is why our aura can reveal so much about us; it is directly linked to massive information databanks within our bodies. Knowing how to read auras is not paranormal or odd. Instead, it can help you uncover hidden issues and problems so you can live a healthier and happier life.

There are certain traits, both weaknesses, and strengths that will always be visible in our auras, think of them like a fingerprint. It is important to know what these are so you can build on your strengths and not let your weaknesses bring you down. Your aura contains this information because whether you want it to or not, these things are part of the vibration and energy that emanates from you. Knowing what to look for in your own aura will help you know what to look for in others since all of the chakra locations are the same, there is always going to be an origin per layer.

We all have habits and patterns, some of which can be traced back to childhood. Unfortunately for us, not all of these are positive. Some of us get trapped in fear by starting negative thoughts that start with "what if" statements, others have a tendency to hold grudges and are unable to move on. Well, our auras will also reflect these things as well. These things can distort the soul and mix with your aura, leaving dark spots where there could be light, this is often referred to as astral debris. Even though it is part of us, it does not have to be, and we are capable of releasing our fears and forming new, positive habits and patterns. Energy cannot be destroyed, but it can be changed, that is something to always think about in terms of your aura.

Everyone is born with the gifts needed to read auras; it is just learning to use them when issues arise. There are many obstacles and blocks, many of which created by our own minds that prevent us from doing so. These can be anything from a fear of failure to working against our own personal abilities. There are many different techniques and combinations of techniques that allow someone to read auras. If you feel as though you are working hard, but having little results, try switching to something that works better for you. Not everyone will receive information in the same way, and there is nothing wrong with that. Your journey is unique to you and knowing what works best for you is part of it. So, if you are not seeing colors, but are receiving images or symbols, or vice versa, learn to work with and interpret what you are being given.

Reading auras can be a practical and useful tool. Some companies even use aura readers for potential employees because a person's aura will reveal whether or not they tend towards cruelty, deception, or violence. Nearly all of our behaviors leave a map on our aura; experienced aura readers can also tell if someone has a drug addiction because of that also leaves a mark. It also works the other way too; it is a wonderful way to see the good hidden in people. Some people are just naturally shy and more closed off, but their aura shows that they are kind, talented individuals.

Knowing auras can feel as complicated as learning a new language, but in the end, it is worth it since it is almost like a key to a new world. Not only does it give you the chance to get to know yourself better, but it gives you the opportunity to see others in a deeper, more meaningful way. Knowing how to use auras to your benefit will help you live a healthier life. In _Auras: Tips and Tricks for Reading People and Energy Fields_, I explain, in further detail, the effects specific behaviors and emotions have on an aura. However, that doesn't mean that based on the information given to you thus far, that you can't do some things to help your aura stay bright. For instance, you know that your aura reflects your physical health, so to make that layer bright, it would only make sense to eat healthy and exercise to be as healthy as you can be. Another example would be that you know dark spots can appear from holding onto fears and negative past experiences, so it is a good idea to let them go and focus on the positive.

One of the best ways to know your own aura is to dedicate some time reading it for yourself. Set aside some time as often as you can to give your aura some attention, see what your strengths and weaknesses are. Over time you will be able to control more of your thoughts and hopefully focusing most of your time and energy on the positive than the negative, which will then be reflected in your aura.

Remember to have fun and appreciate your unique journey. It is easy to lose sight of what is important when you are working towards a goal, but try not to let this desire be one of those times. You are going to learn so much about yourself and others that it should be enjoyable and there should many small successes for you to celebrate along the way. So be patient, trust yourself, and enjoy yourself.

Auras

Tips and Tricks to Reading People and Energy Fields

By Valerie W. Holt

Introduction

Congratulations on downloading *Auras: Tips and Tricks to Reading People and Energy Fields* and thank you for doing so.

The following chapters will discuss the different colors of auras and their meanings. The effects of fear and stress have on auras, and ways to protect your aura from these harmful effects will also be discussed.

There are plenty of books on this subject on the market, thanks again for choosing this one! Every effort was made to ensure it is full of as much useful information as possible; please enjoy!

Chapter 1

Aura Color Meanings

There are seven different layers to the human aura, all of which correspond to a certain chakra. These connections were discussed in the first book Auras: Essential Beginner's Guide to Seeing, Feeling, and Knowing, however, the related colors of each layer and chakra were not discussed. Each chakra and layer is already associated with a color, and healers believe that it is when these colors become muddled or out of balance that the body is suffering.

Layers and Their Colors

(Layer one is closest to the body.)

- Layer 1: The color red and the etheric body.
- Layer 2: The color orange and the emotional body.

48

- Layer 3: The color yellow and the mental body.

- Layer 4: The color green and the astral body.

- Layer 5: The color blue and archetypal body.

- Layer 6: The color indigo and the angelic body.

- Layer 7: The color violet and the ketheric body.

Even though these colors are associated with certain layers and chakras, it does not mean that all auras will contain them. Most people have one color that dominates their aura with some other colors mixed in. Current circumstances and experiences influence the color of an aura and being out of balance is incredibly common. This means that the colors normally associated with a certain layer are being overtaken by another color that is associated with current thoughts, emotions, or even an illness.

Color meanings are complex since there are enveloping personality traits based on the color, but then there are also specific meanings depending on the shade. So, it is important to know all the colors; shades included when doing a reading. For instance, if you see a mostly purple aura, but also some shades of red and green, but you only choose to discuss the purple, you will not be giving an accurate and thorough reading. Just as auras themselves are complex, so too are the meanings behind them. The chakras, and therefore auras, hold so much information, it would be too vague and generic to only focus on one color and ignore and the many different shades and meanings that could reveal so much more.

Color Meanings

Red – Individuals with a red aura are energetic and always looking for their next adventure. They are adventurous with sexual partners, food, and travel, but also quick to get angry which can often cause problems. They are also known to have a bad temper but can be very generous with their energy and time when asked for help. Those with red auras are strong both in mind and body and do not get sick often. Because of their physical nature, they tend to excel at sports and get bored easily. They are also known for starting projects and not finishing them due to a short attention span. They thrive on competition and enjoy winning; this usually means they are very successful in life. However, they do not like being told what to do and are happiest being their own boss.

Red is related to the physical body, such as the circulation and the heart.

- Deep Red – Realistic, survival-oriented, strong-willed, and realistic.
- Muddied Red – Aggression and anger.
- Clear Red – Passionate, sexual, energetic, powerful, and competitive.

Pink – A dominant pink aura means a person is very giving and loving. They prefer to be surrounded by family and friends and enjoy receiving love just as much as they like giving it. They tend to be healthy and active, paying close attention to what they put into their bodies. Those with pink auras are romantic, loyal, and faithful. These individuals are natural healers and are in tune with the needs of others. They need and enjoy creative outlets such as poetry or painting. They are not assertive in nature and will shy away from conflict, but worry about those in need, even going as far as making personal sacrifices to help others. Pink aura people have high standards for themselves and expect the same from others; this includes strong morals and values.

- Bright pink – Sensual, sensitive, artistic, loving, and tender.
- Dark pink – Dishonest and immature.

Orange – Those whose aura is mostly orange are social and generous individuals. They are comfortable being the center of attention or blending in. They are good at picking out gifts for others because of their generous nature. People with an orange aura are also in tune with others' emotions and are very good at sensing both pain and joy in others. They can also be very charming, but also hot-tempered and stubborn. They make great friends and do not hold grudges if a sincere apology is offered. They are confident in all aspects of their lives and tend to lead successful, happy lives. They also tend to make decisions without thinking about the consequences; these rash decisions often lead them into unhealthy personal relationships.

Orange is related to emotions and the reproductive organs.

- Red-orange – Creative power and confidence.

- Orange-yellow – Intelligent, perfectionism, attention to detail, and scientific.

Yellow – Those with a yellow aura are very intelligent and analytical, they make great teachers, scientists, and inventors because of this. However, their work ethic can get out of control causing them to become workaholics which makes it difficult for them to maintain healthy personal relationships. They are fine with their own company and do not get lonely, but are prone to mental pressures which can cause them to become even more withdrawn or depressed. They are inspiring individuals and are confident speaking about their ideas in front of large crowds. Yellow aura people are also good at reading people and have an above average sense of perception. They choose their friends wisely and tend to gravitate towards people who are as smart and witty as they are. To others, they seem to be eccentric with strange hobbies or interests. They are unconventional and unorthodox thinkers, who generally choose to follow their brain instead of their heart. They can also be incredibly critical of both themselves and others.

Yellow is related to life energy and the spleen.

- Pale yellow – Spiritual awareness, hopefulness, and optimism.
- Bright yellow – Struggle for power and fear losing respect, prestige, or control.
- Gold – Inspiring and deep spiritual energy.
- Dark yellow – Student, stressed, lost time, and overly analytical.

Green – People with a green aura are very hard working and creative who strive for perfection in all aspects of their lives. They are grounded and do not need outlandish dreams to bring color or life into their world. Their creativity is usually in the form of decorating, gardening, or cooking since they like practicality so much. However, they also have an eye for beauty, and this shows through in every part of their life, from their clothes to their home, where their belongings are beautiful while still being practical. They are usually very popular, respected, and admired, this is one of the reasons they are usually so successful in business. They think their decisions through and value balance, stability, and security. Green aura people are also healthy, active, and love the outdoors.

Green is related to the lungs and the heart.

- Bright green – Love-centered and a healer.
- Yellow-green – Communicative and creative.
- Forest green – Resentment, jealousy, lack of understanding, and too sensitive.
- Turquoise – Therapist, sensitive, and compassionate.

Blue – Auras that are completely blue are rare, but are usually the strongest color in people with strong personalities. Those with predominantly blue auras are wonderful communicators; they make great poets, writers, and politicians. They are also very intelligent and intuitive. They also have a balance between head and heart when making decisions. Blue aura people are also peacekeepers and have the natural ability to calm angry situations or people. They prefer honesty and directness but can become neglectful of personal relationships by taking on too much.

Blue is related to the thyroid and the throat.

- Soft blue – Clarity, peace, and truth.
- Royal blue – Generous, clairvoyant, and spiritual.
- Dark blue – Fear of expression, the future, or the truth.

Purple – Having a predominantly purple aura is also rather rare, and these people are thought of as incredibly private and mysterious. They have a curious, intuitive mind, and they love to learn.

They never stop asking questions and exploring the world around them. They are not very social and have a small group of friends, they also tend to be unlucky in love, but when they find who they consider being the one, they are devoted and loyal. Purple aura people are very in tune with animals and can sense their emotions, which often leads them to take in strays.

Purple is related to the crown of the head and the nervous system.

- Indigo – Deep feeling, psychic, related to the third eye, and intuitive.
- Lavender – Daydreamer, imaginative, etheric, and visionary.

Silver/white – Those with a silver aura are very gifted, but do not always use these gifts in the best ways. They are considered to be very attractive, talented, and charming. Many people would call them "lucky people." They are successful and choose their friends carefully. Silver aura people are also very intelligent and have an innate psychic ability and are spiritual in nature.

Silver and white are related to both physical and spiritual abundance.

- Metallic silver – Nurturing, intuitive, and open-minded.
- Grey – Accumulated fear and health problems.
- White flashes – Current or future pregnancy.
- Solid white – Reflection, truth, and purity.

Gold – Those who have a gold aura like to be surrounded by luxury and enjoy being the center of attention. They thrive on attracting as much attention and affection from others as possible and can do this easily because they are also very attractive. They are generous with their affection, time, and love as long as they feel it is reciprocated. They are very charismatic and make great listeners. They tend to take too much joy in impressing people and hate to have any of their flaws exposed. They are very independent and hate to ask for help.

Gold is related to protection and enlightenment.

Brown – Generally people do not have a brown aura, but when they do it suggests they are very confused and discouraged about their place in life.

- Light brown – Insecurity and unwillingness to let go.

Black – A black aura is also rare for someone to have, and if they do it usually means they are depressed or very ill.

- Black spots – Health problems, unreleased grief, and consumed light.

Every color has a general set of characteristics and then more specific meanings based on the shade. It is thought that if someone has a rainbow aura, then they are a spiritual healer because this is very difficult to achieve and takes years of practice and discipline. Most of us will have an aura that is mostly one color with other colors faintly spread throughout. So, to get an accurate reading you would need to combine the meanings with one another based on their corresponding color along with the dominant color personality characteristics to get a correct reading.

This might seem difficult at first, but the best person to practice on is yourself, after all, you know yourself best. After you use the mirror to see or feel your own aura, make notes of the colors you see and where and then write up your own reading of yourself. Try to be as thorough as possible, and if it seems like you forgot something, feel free to go back and look again, this is how you learn.

You might be surprised to read what some of the colors meant. Reading your own aura gives you a firsthand look at how much information your aura really retains and shows to those who can see it. As you continue to read your own aura, you will also see it change daily with your mood and thoughts. This is fascinating because it shows you just how much the universe depends on and utilizes change. The energy that you saw yesterday has completely changed today, just from a shift in your thoughts and emotions, because that is how powerful vibrations are.

Chapter 2

The Effect Fear has on Auras

Whether we realize it, or not, fear has always been a large part of our lives, for instance, fear of letting our parents down, fear of authority, and fear of failure. At times, we live our lives in a constant state of perpetual fear. Fear is used to control people, but many people will move away from or grow out of that constant feeling of fear as they lead happy and successful lives. Not everyone is that lucky, sometimes a traumatic event leaves a small amount of lingering fear in its wake that builds and builds, and before you know it, you feel like you can't take a breath. Another example would be working two jobs, but still not making ends meet and being scared each day that your house might be foreclosed on, or you won't have enough money to feed your children. This type of fear, the kind that nags and eats away at you is harmful to your aura.

The kind of fear you have from riding a roller coaster or going on a job interview is positive fear, which is different. If there is even a hint of excitement mixed with the fear, then it will not affect the aura in the same way as the previously mentioned fear will. This is actually referred to as eustress, and it is not haunting, in fact, it is the opposite because it has a beginning and an end. Overpowering and overwhelming fear does not. There is no end, that is why it can be so bleak and cause so many long-term negative effects.

Fear has the power to change the color of your aura completely and shift the focus from chakra to another. This can change your vibrational energy completely, meaning that your aura would be completely different than it was the day before you were crippled with fear. Remember, some experiences and events leave a permanent mark on our auras, you don't want one of those marks to be fear because it will be even more difficult to overcome if that were the case. Fear and stress is something that can be overcome, but what is worrisome is what that fear and stress manifest over time.

Fear is a strong emotion, and as we know the aura is a reflection of this, so when the dominant emotion is fear, the three lower chakras would be the most central forces in our aura. This means we would be constantly worried about survival matters such as money, sexual issues, and ego. Our top three chakras, which deal with spirituality, creativity, and optimism would be mostly left out. This would lead to a murky and muddled aura, meaning there is very little joy and happiness in our life because fear takes up too much space and energy.

Fear wreaks havoc on the nervous system which hinders your ability to connect to the spiritual realm and the body's ability to cope with stress. Depending on your main aura color and your personality type, living in a state of fear can cause someone to become clinically depressed, withdrawn, and in some cases, extremely ill. If it gets to this point, the aura is full of dark black holes or spaces, making it obvious that there is a problem. Your aura always holds the potential of recovering, but sometimes convincing our own brain of that is what makes things so difficult.

Living in fear like this will only make life more difficult because other people would be less likely to gravitate towards you, making you feel even more alone and scared. The aura is like a magnet, and it will continue to attract energy, just like those around you. This means that until you can release the fear, it will continue to snowball until it is overwhelming and you feel as though you are suffocating. This is a vicious cycle that will only darken your aura even more. Those around you will also attract your negative energy, so you would also be indirectly harming those around you with your negative energy since their auras are like magnets too.

One of the most common reasons for this type of fear is a lack of money for basic necessities. So, it is thought that if you were to take someone who lives in fear for this reason and put them in an environment where money does not exist, their aura would immediately shift to the higher chakras. This would mean that they would be happier and their aura would reflect that. The theory is that by completely removing the problem, you have also completely removed the fear. While, this does hold some merit, because one of the best things to do in life is to remove negative energy, this example is just completely unrealistic.

We live in the real world, and we know that money does exist, just like egos do. So, completely getting rid of the problem is not an option, after all, there are only so many hours you can work in a week. One of the best things to do for this is to ask for help and come up with a plan to reduce some of the stress, and therefore the feeling of fear. Sometimes, all it takes is some financial planning to make a difference or for someone to deliver a rude awakening in the form of harsh criticism. Regardless of the problem, there are many different solutions, and part of releasing fear is training your brain to stop jumping to the worst-case scenario. Our own brains can be the source of so much of our fears and stressors, simply because some of us are more prone to worrying than others, or we accidentally make up fears that our body and brain perceive as real threats. Ending this vicious cycle is not easy, but it is possible and using your own aura as a measure of success can be very useful.

This can be done because energy cannot be destroyed, only changed. The energy that already exists that is being wasted on fear can be changed to something more positive. This makes it unnecessary to destroy it since it is possible to change it into something that will help you. This sounds so easy, but until you learn to control your thoughts, this task feels almost impossible. That is why it is important to be as self-aware as possible. The more you know about yourself and the source of your fear, the more likely you will be able to find some positive energy to focus on. The universe is energy and because energy and vibrations are always changing, so too will an aura. Take comfort in the fact that nothing is permanent and it is never too late for an aura to change.

Every decision you make and thought you put out into the universe has repercussions. Thoughts of fear and stress are only going to lead to more fear and stress until the cycle is successfully broken. Your aura is a reflection of what you think and feel, and if it always has the potential of changing, then that means so does the rest of you.

Chapter 3

How to Protect Your Aura

Now that you know what the aura is made of and that it is a direct reflection of your thoughts and feelings, you might feel the need to protect it. The good news is, even if your aura is full of gray colors and maybe even some black spots, it is possible to make a complete turnaround. Our aura can change as fast as our minds can, and often does. Of course, some general characteristics remain the same, as you learned in the other book, *Auras: Essential Beginner's Guide to Seeing, Feeling, and Knowing*.

The more sensitive and empathic you are the more important it is for you to clean and protect your aura. These types are more vulnerable to the harmful effects of energies than those who are less sensitive. However, everyone can benefit from cleaning and protecting their aura.

Ways to Protect Your Aura:

1. Bubble – This is one of the most common and effective ways of protecting your aura from negative energies and influences. Most people perform daily when they wake up in the morning, but how often and when you choose to do it is up to you. This is a good habit to get into because not only does it help to protect your aura, it also helps connect you to the universe.

    Imagine a white light coming down through the crown of your head, entering through your head and then falls down all the way to your feet. Visualize it creating a giant white light barrier or bubble that is surrounding you and your entire aura. White is pure and protective, but you can change the color if you think one suits your needs better. You can also visualize symbols and items that you think would help protect your aura. For instance, mirrors that would deflect any negative energy or hearts that would attract love and affection. This is just a way to personalize your bubble to make it work better for your specific needs. Since this is a visualization exercise, you can also modify it based on specific circumstances, like if you know, you must speak in front of a large group or if you are signing divorce papers. The bubble is yours to change and customize based on what you need.

2. You already know that your aura is like a magnet, it will attract energy both negative and positive. Sit down and write a list of all the things in your life that you would consider to be sources of negative energy. It can be anything from a student loan payment to a person who never has anything nice to say. Once you have compiled your list, go through and see which things can be completely removed from your life. This seems harsh and is much easier said than done, but in the end, it will be worth it. You might be surprised at

the number of things that can successfully cut from your life. Obviously, some things must stay, but when confronted with a list, you will be able to see, in black and white, what is bringing you down. Next, of course, you must take action to make the changes you deemed possible and stick to it.

3. This one is connected to the previous method, so let's assume that you did go through and cut out as much negative energy as you could. Now, it is time to replace as much of that as possible with positive energy. Devote time to something that makes you happy, whether it be going out with friends or building a birdhouse. If it makes you happy, do it. So many people forget to set aside time for themselves, and their aura pays the price for this. Get in the habit of setting aside time for yourself.

4. This is also a difficult protection method since it involves doing something that does not come naturally; looking inward to see if we are the source of the negative energy. As humans, we have the power to be our own worst critics, and we have a habit of putting ourselves down. Take some time to focus on how you think about yourself. It's amazing how hard we can be on ourselves without realizing it. If you find yourself getting caught up in a negative thought, find one positive thing to think about, even if it is something tiny. Even the worst days have some type of silver lining, so start looking for those and latching onto them. Set yourself a complaining time or sentence limit and then stop complaining. It is okay to express your displeasure, but it is not okay to dwell on it. Learn to let go of the negativity and move on.

5. The best way to protect your aura is not to do things that will harm it in the first place. The

stronger a person's aura is, the better it will be for not falling prey to negative energies. You know the difference between right and wrong. Make an honest effort at living your best life, and your aura will reflect that. Think your decisions through before you make them, and think about others' needs. Resisting all temptation is not necessary, this doesn't mean live like a saint. It simply means, live the best you can and make the best decisions you can.

How you choose to protect your aura is up to you, but all the methods mentioned are things you can do on your own. Some people suggest going to a healer and having them cleanse your aura, but not everyone has that option. These techniques are universal, and anyone can do them. Some of them might seem easy, but when it comes down to it, you might realize it has been weeks or months since you have taken any time out for yourself. Life tends to get away from us, and that makes it easy to forget to take care of ourselves.

Your aura is still going to act as a magnet, and it will not always be blemish free, but don't punish yourself for it. One of the worst things you can do is dwell on the negative, remember to keep looking for that silver lining. It is healthier to hold onto a tiny positive than it is to hold onto a huge negative. As you move forward on your journey, remember that.

Chapter 4

Psychic Development and Aura Relation

As you become more adept at seeing or feeling auras, you are furthering your psychic development. The two go together, the more you develop your psychic abilities, the more sensitive and empathic you will be, which will allow you to see or feel auras better and stronger. The better you get at feeling or seeing auras, the stronger your psychic ability becomes.

Anything dealing with energies, the mind's eye, the Divine, chakras, or things not felt by the basic senses is going to be grouped under psychic ability. This is not psychic in the traditional sense, there is no fortune-telling when it comes to aura reading, but it does involve vibrations and other realms, so, therefore, falls under the category of psychic ability. This means that if you want to see or feel auras in a stronger manner, the best way to do so is to focus on developing your psychic abilities. Certain abilities come more naturally to some than others, and in the beginning, it is best to foster the abilities that do feel more natural.

Every time you practice reading your own aura, you are furthering your psychic development. Think of it like a muscle, the more you use it, the bigger it will get. Each time you call forth the protective bubble, you would also be flexing the psychic muscle. It's easy to develop our psychic abilities without even realizing it, that is one of the reasons it gets easier to see and feel auras over time. You're learning to depend on a sense that is not one of the basic five. Simply putting faith in your own mind's ability to control its thoughts, such as through meditation, is another way you develop your psychic ability.

Not only does your ability to see and feel auras increase, but the strength of your own aura will too. This happens naturally because your aura contracts and expands based on circumstances, and as psychic ability develops, the more receptive your higher three chakras become, making you more sensitive and intuitive than you already were. This stronger awareness will cause your aura to become brighter and stronger. This is a goal many people share and they focus on making their aura stronger and brighter by developing their innate psychic abilities. For others, it is simply a welcomed side-effect.

Even if you can see or feel auras, you do not have to label yourself a psychic. Everyone is born with the ability to see auras; you have just chosen to learn to do so. So, your psychic ability might be much more developed than the average person, but again, it is your journey, and if you choose not to use the term psychic, that is your choice. The two main ways in which auras are experienced are through the two psychic abilities known as clairvoyance and clairsentience.

Clairvoyance – Able to perceive things or events that go beyond normal sensory contact.

Clairsentience – The ability to feel energy, from nearly all things, such as emotion, pain, and other things that are not seen.

Just like there are many kinds of auras, there are many different types of clairvoyants and clairsentients. Not all of them are going to be able to see or feel auras, and if they do, not all of them are going to experience them in the same way. However, what they do have in common is that to make themselves better at what they do by practice. The same can be said for those attempting to read auras. The more you learn about your specific abilities and the more you learn to use them, the better you will become at aura readings.

Auras are part of our lives, whether we choose to acknowledge them or not. The universe is made of vibrations, and humans are not an exception. It wouldn't be natural for us not to be made up of the same vibrations since we too are part of the universe. We were all born with the ability to witness and experience these vibrations one way or another. More often than not, we just have to get out of our own way to do so.

Other Publications by Author

For more books by Valerie please visit her
Amazon Author Page or go to:

bit.ly/wiccabooks

Empath*: How to Flourish as an Empath & The
Little Known History of Empaths*

Third Eye*: Proven Techniques to Increase
Intuition and Psychic Awareness, Forgotten
History of the Third Eye in the Ancient Americas*

Psychic*: How to Unlock Your Psychic Abilities
and Enhance Intuition*

Witchcraft*: Wicca for Beginner's, Book of
Shadows, Candle Magic, Herbal Magic, Wicca
Altar*

Zodiac Signs*: Character, Essence, and the
Nature of the 12 Zodiac Signs & Relationship
Compatibility Guide*

84624719R00049

Made in the USA
San Bernardino, CA
09 August 2018